Agile Comedy of Errors

A PRACTICAL HANDBOOK FOR YOUR EVERYDAY'S AGILE WORK

SUBRAMANIAN PALANIAPPAN

Made with ♥ on the Notion Press Platform
www.notionpress.com

Contents

Introduction

Why Agile?

In today's rapidly evolving business landscape, the need for agility and flexibility has never been greater. Traditional project management approaches often needed help to keep up with the pace of change, leading to delays, cost overruns, and products that missed the mark. Enter Agile.

Agile methodologies like Scrum and Kanban have revolutionized how teams approach project management and product development. The Agile Manifesto values individuals, working software, collaboration, and responding to change over other traditional measures that are usually the slow-down factors for any project deliverables.

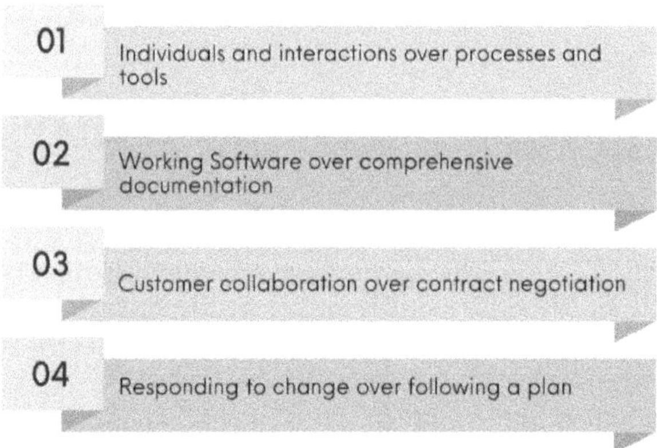

Fig 1: Agile Manifesto

Agile frameworks are a customer-centric approach to software development that aims to provide high-quality software consistently. They are based on a set of 12 principles and values that guide the development process, keeping customers included in all phases of the development. The critical focus of agile methodology is to produce working software continuously. This is achieved through small, incremental changes that can be quickly tested and evaluated by the customer. This approach provides early feedback, allowing the development team to make necessary improvements more efficiently.

Agile methodology has given rise to several key concepts that have become integral to modern software development. These include Shift Left, Fast Feedback-Loops, Fail-Fast Fail-Safe, Design Thinking, Iterative Development, and more. Each concept aims to perfect the development process to ensure highest quality possible.

Shift Left is a process that involves testing software early in the development cycle to find and fix issues before they become bigger problems. Fast feedback loops involve providing rapid feedback to the development team during the development process, helping them make informed decisions. Fail-fast fail-safe is a philosophy that encourages developers to test and fail early, allowing them to learn from their mistakes and create better software. Design Thinking makes the customer at the center of the design process and assure the final product meets their needs. Lastly, iterative development involves continuous testing and refining software to ensure it is of the highest quality possible.

A customer-centric approach emphasizes continuous improvement and rapid feedback has become a standard practice for most organizations. However, implementing these frameworks still presents some challenges. Despite these challenges, agile frameworks are currently the most widely adopted method for software companies that need faster deliveries and customer focus.

Purpose of the Book

While Agile offers a powerful framework for success, the journey to becoming truly Agile is not without its challenges. Many teams and organizations need help with common misconceptions and pitfalls when implementing Agile practices. This book aims to shed light on these challenges, offering insights, discussions, and practical strategies to overcome them.

This book aims to clarify misunderstandings about agile, regardless of your role within the team. Even when software companies transition from traditional methods to agile Ways of Working (WoW), they still face challenges in changing their mindset. This book will assist you in addressing some of the questions that come up in your daily work life.

How to Use This Book

This book is intended for individuals who have a fundamental understanding of Agile methodologies like Scrum and Kanban but meet recurring issues during their implementation. Instead of repeating the basics, we delve into the specific ceremonies and practices, emphasizing common myths and misconceptions.

Each chapter concentrates on a vital aspect of Agile implementation, such as Sprint Planning, Daily Stand-ups, Backlog Refinement, Sprint Reviews, Retrospectives, and more. We address these topics in a conversational manner, providing relatable scenarios, explaining myths, engaging in discussions, and furnishing actionable strategies for improvement.

Whether you're a Scrum Master, Agile Coach, Product Owner, or team member, this book aims to be a pragmatic guide to navigate the intricacies of Agile implementation. It's not merely about averting mistakes but also about adopting Agile principles to encourage collaboration, innovation, and continuous improvement within your teams.

The scrum discussions presented in this book are grounded on the most recent version of the scrum guide released in 2020. If you have previously adopted or have a certification in agile before the release of the 2020 scrum guide, I strongly recommend that you refer to the updated scrum guide, as you may notice a lot of significant changes. The prescriptive part of the guide has mainly been removed, providing you with the freedom to implement the concepts in a manner that suits your organization while ensuring that the agile values and principles are noticed.

Matt and Don will stand for my thoughts from my imaginary team. They are working for Acme Corporation. They will represent the entire team, with Matt possibly sounding like the scrum master most of the time and Don as one of the lead resources within the legacy teams. I deliberately mentioned "lead" to emphasize that the traditional hierarchy remains within Agile teams, which is a myth. Agile team structure only holds Scrum Master, Product Owner, and Developers. Every other stakeholder is included in the project, but these are only the main three characters that may take your Agile journey to success. So, when you read this book, remember that if it resembles your current structure, work to change the legacy style of teams.

A few words from the Author

As someone who has walked the Agile path, I've experienced firsthand the challenges and triumphs of Agile implementation. Through years of working in India and the US with diverse teams and organizations, I've seen the same misconceptions surface repeatedly.

This book is born out of a passion for helping teams unlock the full potential of Agile, avoid common pitfalls, and embrace the spirit of agility in their work. The insights shared here will empower you on your Agile journey, leading to more successful projects, happier teams, and delighted customers.

I have pursued many certifications to improve my work, but unfortunately, my efforts have not been successful due to the team's adherence to non-agile practices. I have authored this book to address this issue that dispels myths in specific areas you may meet daily. The language used in these books is simple and relatable to subjective experiences, making it easy to find instances where they occur in your projects.

The main objective of this book is not to provide a detailed explanation of every single agile ceremony and how to execute it. Instead, the book aims to highlight the common mistakes that occur during agile implementation. Therefore, readers of this book are expected to have a basic understanding of agile principles and the popular frameworks Kanban and Scrum.

I am open to feedback and queries and look forward to discussing these topics further with you. Together, we can embark on an Agile adventure to help us uncover myths, correct misconceptions, and lay a solid foundation for Agile excellence.

Let's get started!

Mother of All Myths - " We do Agile!"

Agile methodology overcomes the limitations found in the traditional project management methods such as Waterfall. Although Waterfall was sometimes effective, its inflexible, linear approach often made it difficult to adapt to changing requirements and market dynamics. Agile, on the other hand, prioritizes flexibility, collaboration, and iterative development. It recognizes that the ability to respond quickly to feedback and evolving needs is crucial in today's fast-paced business environment. Agile methodologies promote incremental delivery of working software, enabling continuous improvement and adaptation throughout the project lifecycle. This approach allows for the efficient and effective delivery of value to stakeholders, fostering innovation, and reducing the risk of project failure. Moreover, Agile methodologies emphasize close collaboration between cross-functional teams and stakeholders, promoting transparency, communication, and shared ownership of project goals. By embracing Agile principles and practices, organizations can better navigate uncertainty, optimize resource allocation, and ultimately deliver higher-quality products that meet customer needs and expectations in a rapidly changing world.

In contrast to the Waterfall approach, Agile methodologies prioritize customer collaboration and early delivery of working software. By involving the customer from day one and continuously soliciting feedback throughout the development process, Agile ensures that the product evolves in alignment with the customer's changing needs and preferences. This iterative approach not only allows for greater flexibility and responsiveness to customer requirements but also minimizes the risk of costly rework or misalignment between the final product and customer expectations. Agile's focus on delivering incremental value and engaging customers in co-creation fosters a more dynamic and adaptive approach to project management, better suited to today's rapidly evolving business landscape.

The common misunderstanding about Agile is that it solely consists of a set of ceremonies and sprints, a superficial acceptance of its practices, and often falls short of the true Agile principles. Many organizations believe conducting Daily Stand-ups, Sprint Planning, Sprint Reviews, and Retrospectives is enough to be considered Agile. Still, this approach is often insufficient to fully embrace Agile principles.

A common symptom of this myth is the practice of a "sprint-based waterfall" where teams perform activities sequentially within sprints. For instance, in one sprint, they concentrate on requirements; in the next sprint, they tackle architecture and design, followed by development, testing, etc. This mimics the waterfall approach but with timeboxes.

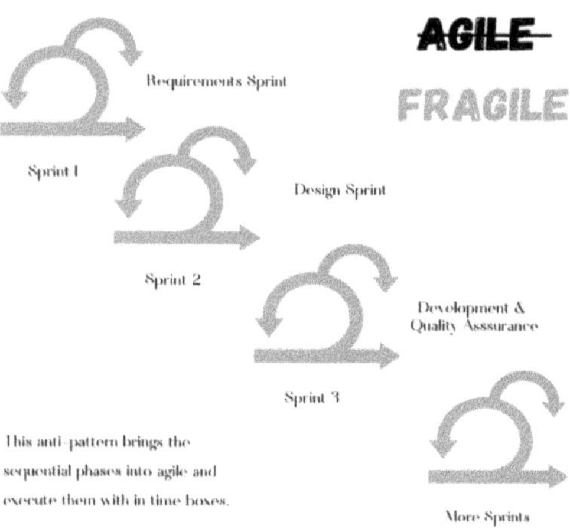

Fig 2 - sprint-based waterfall

Another symptom is the need for more adaptability and responsiveness to change. Teams may view Agile as a rigid process where each sprint must be planned in advance, leaving little room for adjustments based on feedback and evolving requirements.

Matt is an experienced project manager who is passionate

about the principles of Agile methodology. Recently, the organization adopted Agile methodology as the new way of working, and Matt attended organizational-wide training programs to learn more about it. As part of his role, he helps others embrace Agile methodology.

Don is a new hire in the business who is eager to learn more about Agile methodology. However, he is confused by some of the misconceptions surrounding its implementation. Therefore, Matt and Don decided to meet frequently to discuss these myths and learn how to embrace Agile methodology in their projects.

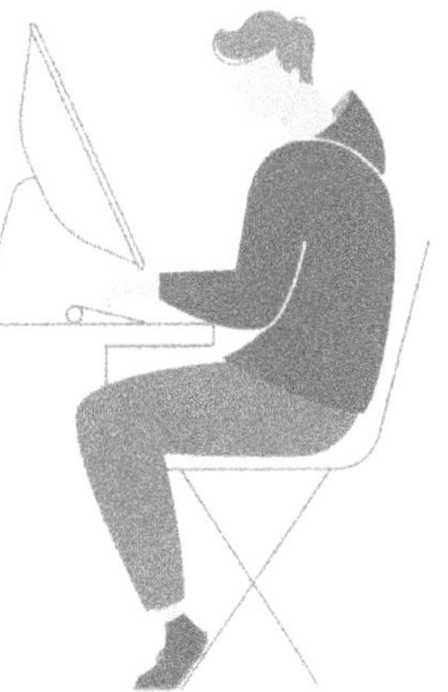

Matt and Don meet at a bustling café for lunch.

Matt: *Hey, Don, thanks for meeting up today. I thought it would be good to chat about Agile, especially since you're starting on projects here.*

Don: *Absolutely, Matt. I've been reading it, but I keep hearing conflicting things about "doing Agile" versus "embracing Agile." It's a bit confusing.*

Matt: *I understand what you mean. There's a myth that just following Agile practices by the book is all you need. But really, it's about embracing the Agile mindset.*

Don: *Ah, so it's not just about ticking off boxes on a checklist?*

Matt: *Exactly. Let me explain it this way. Doing Agile is like going through the motions—holding daily stand-ups, having a backlog, doing sprints. However, embracing Agile is about understanding why we do these things and the values behind them.*

Don: *So, it's more about philosophy than mechanics?*

Matt: *Absolutely. Take the daily stand-ups, for example. It's not just a status update meeting. It's about team communication, collaboration, and quick problem-solving.*

Don: *Ah, I see. It's about fostering that team spirit and adaptability.*

Matt: *Right on. Also, embracing Agile means being open to change. It's about responding to customer feedback quickly, even if it means adjusting our plans mid-sprint.*

Don: *That makes sense. So, it's not about sticking to a rigid plan but being flexible and responsive.*

Matt: *Exactly! Agile isn't a one-size-fits-all solution. It's about finding what works best for our team and our project.*

Don: *I'm starting to get a clearer picture now. It's not just a methodology; it's a mindset shift.*

Matt: *Spot on, Don. The more we embrace that mindset, the more successful our Agile projects will be.*

Don: *Thanks, Matt. This conversation has cleared things up for me. I'm excited to dive deeper into Agile with this new perspective.*

Matt: *Anytime, Don. I'm glad we could chat about it. Agile is all about learning and growing together.*

Matt and Don discussed mindset concerning individuals. However, a cultural shift is more crucial for organizations than an individual mindset. In simpler terms, a mindset change can be considered part of a cultural shift in an organization.

Agile principles challenge traditional hierarchical structures, which can be a significant shift from the traditional command-and-control management style. Agile promotes self-organizing teams, shared ownership, and collaboration across roles, but many organizations hesitate to embrace these principles in their entirety.

Several root causes of this reluctance include fear of change, a lack of understanding of Agile principles and their value, preserving the status quo, and short-term thinking. For instance, some organizations focus solely on the immediate benefits of Agile, such as faster delivery or better visibility into project progress, and need to see the long-term advantages of improved adaptability, increased customer satisfaction, and a sustainable pace of work.

Reducing Agile to a set of ceremonies without a true Agile culture may limit the delivery of value to customers, lead to an increased risk of project failure, cause stagnation and inefficiency, and result in employee frustration. To break this myth, organizations should invest in educating all levels of the organization about Agile principles and values, encourage a cultural shift towards collaboration, transparency, and continuous improvement, trust teams to make decisions and self-organize around work, encourage experimentation with different practices, gather feedback, and continuously improve, break down silos between teams, departments, and hierarchical levels to promote shared goals and collective success and keep the focus on delivering value to customers.

Throughout this book, let's dive deep into most areas where common mistakes happen due to several factors.

CHAPTER 1

Sprint Planning

"We Must Plan Every Detail Before Starting"

Sprint Planning is an essential ceremony where the team collaborates to decide the backlog items they will work on during the upcoming sprint. However, the team's goal is to plan only some minute tasks to completion. Instead, they should focus on understanding the sprint goal, selecting the highest priority items, and creating a plan, allowing flexibility and adaptation as the work progresses.

The presence of the three main roles in Agile -Product Owner, Scrum Master, and Development Team- ensures a comprehensive understanding and alignment of objectives. Their active engagement and collaboration breathe life into the planning process, fostering a sense of shared ownership and commitment. A critical interlude in this orchestration session is the careful review and refinement of the Product Backlog. Here, stories are not merely discussed but lovingly scrutinized, refined, and clarified. This exercise, in detail, ensures that each user story and its corresponding acceptance criteria are well-understood and agreed upon by the team. This harmonious tuning of the backlog not only sets the stage for a successful sprint but also serves as a touchstone for the team's shared understanding of the project's trajectory.

There is a common misconception about Sprint Planning that suggests the team must plan every single detail of the upcoming sprint before starting work. This myth might originate from the project's desire for certainty and predictability. However, Agile frameworks like Scrum prioritize adaptability and responsiveness to change, which this myth can hinder.

Matt and Don met at the cafe vending machine today, which was the day of the sprint planning at Acme Corporation. Matt started a conversation to check if everything was for the sprint planning session. Listen to them.

Matt: *Hey Don, it's time for our Sprint Planning meeting. Are we ready for the session?*

Don: *Absolutely, Matt! I've broken down every task, estimated the hours, and created a detailed Gantt chart for the sprint.*

Matt: *Don, were all the developers present when these were completed? I don't recall a refinement session where we did all these.*

Don: *Oh, I thought we needed to have everything planned out to ensure we stay on track, so I just did it myself. No, I didn't include them. We will discuss it in the planning session anyway, won't we?*

Matt: *It's great that you've put in the effort, but it would be a good idea if we included everyone in the process. Also, you don't need to work in silo to get things done beforehand, Don. We are still determining if we have met all the requirements comprehensively.*

Don: *I see what you mean. So, how do we strike the right balance during Sprint Planning?*

Matt: *We should focus on understanding the sprint goal, selecting the most important backlog items, and creating a flexible adjustment plan. Let's make sure our plan leaves room for unexpected tasks or priority changes.*

- Ensure everyone on the team understands the primary goal of the sprint (Sprint Goal). This will aid in task prioritization and decision-making throughout the sprint.
- At least once a week, the entire team gets together in the refinement meeting to fine-tune the stories for upcoming sprints. The meeting involves a detailed discussion of the requirements and the addition of tasks. In addition, the team estimates the tasks to be at a high level during the meeting.

- Adopt a "just-in-time" planning approach instead of planning every single detail upfront. Plan enough to start and refine the plan as more information becomes available.
- Encourage the team to define tasks at a level that provides clarity without going into unnecessary detail. This will allow for easier adaptation if priorities shift.
- Have frequent check-ins during the sprint to review progress, adjust plans if necessary, and solve any possible obstacles. Remember that Sprint Goal stays the same unless the goal has adjustments by the Product Owner's approval.
- Remind the team that change is a natural part of the Agile process and to be receptive to it. Being open to change and adjusting plans accordingly is crucial to success.

✓ Watch your workplace

↷ Watch if traditional team hierarchy with one person authority still exists. In this way only a few people decide what should happen, and others just follow the path with no vision.

↱ Planning is beneficial only if everyone is involved, preferably in a refinement meeting where they can express their ideas and concerns. If not, this is an area that requires attention to improve.

↱ While it may not be necessary to have a complete plan, it is still important to have a backlog of stories, ideally with a few rounds of refinement already completed. This ensures that the planning session takes place without any surprises.

↱ Capacity planning should not be overlooked before accepting stories. Without it, how can you measure the amount of work that can be accepted?

Sprint planning is one of the essential ceremonies. During this ceremony, the team picks up refined stories and accepts them to the current sprint based on their capacity. The Scrum Master steers the team to meet the planning goals and ensures that the team has enough work for the sprint.

It is advisable not to distribute the entire team's bandwidth while planning. It would be ideal to keep a buffer (20%—30 %) for developers, which they can use for unplanned activities, meetings, and demos.

It is important to remember that sprint planning is not a one-time event. Several factors can lead to scope creep, such as changes in market needs, stakeholder preferences, business requirements, security or compliance needs, etc. In such cases, an ad hoc sprint planning meeting may be necessary to accommodate the newly introduced scope. During this meeting, all team members come together to assess the potential impact of the added scope on the sprint goal and find any potential slippage in the deadline. The team may also consider descoping some of the existing work with the Product Owner's approval to ensure the sprint goal is still achievable.

Alternatively, if the entire sprint scope needs to be changed, the sprint planning meeting becomes a planning session for a new set of scopes by canceling the current sprint. Although canceling a sprint is uncommon, changing the entire sprint goal is possible. However, the ultimate focus is always to deliver the sprint goal that has been agreed upon with the business, and the team is still motivated to achieve this goal. Therefore, it is important to conduct regular sprint planning meetings and to be prepared to adapt to changing circumstances as necessary.

CHAPTER 2

Daily Stand-ups (Scrum) / Daily Kanban Meetings

"It's Just a Status Update Meeting"

The Daily Stand-up, or Daily Meetings in Kanban, is often misconstrued. Many assume it to be a regular status update where team members answer three questions: "What did you do yesterday?" "What are you doing today?" and "Do you have any blockers?" Although these questions are part of the agenda, the true purpose of this daily practice is far more significant.

> It's worth noting that the significant change in Scrum Guide 2020 allows us to adjust daily stand-up meetings to suit our needs. So, we don't need to stick to the same pattern of Daily Stand-Up meetings asking the famous three questions. Make amendments as they fit your organization, but remember to keep the meeting productive and collaborative.

The Daily Stand-up offers a crucial opportunity for the team to collaborate, synchronize, and find potential obstacles early on. It is not only a list of tasks completed or planned by each team member, but it also offers a chance to share insights, offer help, and work collectively towards achieving the sprint goal.

The Scrum methodology implementation protocols have been significantly updated in the Scrum Guide 2020. Unlike earlier versions, the guidebook no longer requires specific practices. Consequently, the traditional three questions asked during the Daily Scrum are no longer mandatory. However, the fundamental principles of Scrum remain unchanged. Teams can still follow the traditional three-question format if it works for them, or they can make modifications to suit their specific needs.

The Scrum framework emphasizes regular team communication and collaboration to achieve goals. It is paramount to keep communication channels open, and any obstacles that could hinder the team's progress must be found and addressed promptly. Although the Scrum Guide 2020 does not mandate specific protocols, adhering to the fundamental principles and values of Scrum is essential to ensure that the team is working efficiently and effectively.

Matt: *Good morning, Don! Ready for our Daily Stand-up?*

Don: *Morning, Matt! Absolutely. I'll just get my update ready: yesterday, I worked on fixing the login issue, today I'll be testing the new feature and that's it.*

Matt: *Sounds good. It's important to know what everyone's up to. But remember, it's more than just a status update. Any obstacles you're facing that we should discuss?*

Don: *Actually, now that you mention it, I did run into a problem with the new API integration. I might need some help figuring it out.*

Matt: *Got it. Thanks for bringing that up. We'll make sure to address it after the meeting. Anything else we should be aware of?*

Don: *Yeah, I'll be out of the office for a couple of days next week. I want to give everyone heads up and check if anyone has any dependencies on me, so I can sort them out before I leave.*

Matt: *This is great, thank you for bringing it up, Don! It will help me adjust any dates according to your plans, as well as others who may be affected.*

PO: *Hey, are there any potential delays or adjustments to our sprint goal? If yes, I am open to reviewing.*

Don: *No issues, Mr. PO. I have already taken care of the deliverables, which won't impact our sprint goals.*

Matt: *Alright then, let's move on ...*

The above conversation is an example of a typical conversation between a scrum master and a developer during a daily scrum meeting. It is important to note that this is just an example, and in a mature agile environment, the scrum master will not need to moderate this meeting. Instead, someone on the team can randomly start the meeting each day, and the person who completes their update will then choose the next person to share their updates.

The scrum master assures the team stays focused and on track during the meeting. If the conversation starts to go off-topic, the scrum master will step in to bring it back on track. If you have any action items or require further clarification, you can always set up another meeting with the necessary stakeholders for a more specific discussion.

It is important to note that it is not the scrum master's responsibility to set up these additional meetings. As a team member, you must ensure that your deliverables are on track. The scrum master will only intervene if there are impediments, cross-team deliverables, or dependencies with other teams.

Consider changing the location each time to increase

engagement during the daily scrum meeting. While it was once recommended that the meeting be conducted in the same place every time, it is no longer necessary. You could meet at a coffee shop, a nearby garden, or even just take a walk while discussing. Make sure to choose a location where there are no distractions. If the team is more engaged while moving around, trying different locations is an innovative idea. It is important to note that the Agile philosophy originally supported co-located teams, but due to the pandemic, most teams have switched to a hybrid model. Therefore, we must adapt whatever works best and is most effective for our team.

To improve standup meetings, consider these tactics to drop anti-patterns within the team.

✓ Watch your workplace

↪ Daily Scrum takes longer, and everyone discusses their status updates in detail. Bring them to focus.

> ↪ No dashboard or sprint boards are kept open when the team discuss their updates. This leads to discussion with no reference points.
>
> ↪ A few people stay silent, claiming that everything is going well. However, it's important to review their work at once following the stand-up call to avoid any hidden surprises.

- **Focus on Obstacles**: Encourage team members to highlight real obstacles or challenges. This opens the door for collaboration and problem-solving within the team.
- **Offer Help**: If someone mentions a blocker, offer immediate aid instead of just noting it down or finding someone to help resolve it. The Scrum master ensures that the person who reported a blocker and the one who offered help will meet after the stand-up call without fail.
- **Keep It Relevant**: Ensure that discussions during the Stand-up focus on sprint goals and tasks that affect the team.
- **Limit Time**: Stand-ups should be concise and time-boxed to prevent them from becoming lengthy status meetings. The ideal duration can be 15 minutes for a team size of 10 or below.

It is not mandatory for the Scrum Master to lead the daily Scrum meetings. A round-robin approach can be used, where each team member takes turns daily. This helps in promoting the adoption of the agile among everyone, leading to a more " Being Agile" environment.

CHAPTER 3

Backlog Refinement

"Refinement Is Optional"

Backlog refinement is regularly updating product backlogs with new requirements, enhancing the already drafted stories, and aligning the priorities so top priority items stay on top for teams to pick up the work.

Backlog Refinement is an important aspect of Agile frameworks that is often misunderstood. While some believe that it is an optional ceremony, it is, in fact, an essential process that ensures the smooth running of Agile projects. Neglecting Backlog Refinement can lead to a backlog filled with outdated, unclear, or irrelevant items, which can significantly impact the project's outcome.

The purpose of Refinement session is to ensure that the product backlog is updated, prioritized, and ready for upcoming sprints. This involves refining user stories, breaking down large items into smaller, more manageable tasks, estimating the time and effort required for each task, and adjusting priorities based on changing requirements or feedback.

Refining user stories involves ensuring that they accurately reflect the stakeholders' needs and expectations and are written in a way the development team can understand. Breaking down large items into smaller tasks helps ensure that each item can be completed within the sprint's timeframe and that the team clearly understands what is expected of them.

Estimating tasks is a critical part of Backlog Refinement, as it helps the team to identify potential roadblocks and determine how much work can be accomplished in each sprint. Adjusting priorities based on changing requirements or feedback ensures the product backlog remains relevant and aligned with the overall project goals.

When estimating project deliverables, we use story points. It is important to note that no direct relationship between story points and time exists. However, the industry has proved a standard by assigning a particular time limit for each story point size. This approach works well when dealing with quantifiable tasks that can generate meaningful metrics at the end of each sprint.

> Story Points have no correlation with time. However; assigning time limits to each story point size helps during early agile adoption. Your goal is to move away from time limits and use only Story Points. This will eventually be

achieved when the organization gets matured in Agile practices

Matt: *Hey Don, remember we have a Backlog Refinement session today? Just a reminder, please make it.*

Don: *Oh no, sorry, Matt. I have something important to be taken care of at this time. I figured we could plan as we go, you know? Agile and all that.*

Matt: *I get where you're coming from, but neglecting Backlog Refinement might lead to some surprises down the road.*

Don: *Surprises? Like what?*

Matt: *Well, imagine we start a sprint and realize halfway through that some user stories are vague, others are duplicated, and a few are no longer relevant. It could throw off our entire plan.*

Don: *Hmm, I see your point. But isn't Refinement just adding more meetings to our already busy schedule?*

Matt: *It's more than just a meeting, Don. Think of it as tending to a garden. We want to ensure our backlog is healthy, with clear, prioritized items that align with our product goals.*

Don: *Alright, how do we make Backlog Refinement more effective without feeling like a burden?*

Matt: *Let's schedule regular Refinement sessions where we focus on refining user stories, breaking down large tasks, estimating, and ensuring priorities are clear. This way, our sprints will be smoother, and we'll have a backlog that sets us up for success.*

Don: *That makes sense! But why can't Sara, my lead, provide me with details after the meeting? You know she is the best person to estimate this feature.*

Matt: *You're missing my point. Sara's estimate is based on her understanding of the requirements. But what if you have questions that reveal real-life use cases? Consider this.*

Don: *Gotcha...! I understand it, Matt. I will make it Today for sure. Let's dive deep.*

Listen to this conversation. Don is bringing a traditional hierarchy-based team here. He expects his leader to make decisions without feeling empowered to do so. This not only relinquishes power but also creates bottlenecks where people become overly dependent on each other over time, leading to complex dependencies.

✓ Watch your workplace

- Only a few people are actively taking part, and others stay silent. This may show a lack of empowerment within the team, or it could be that one person is taking the lead, and others are allowing them to play their part as well.
- No formal estimation technique, such as planning poker, is used. The team discusses and arrives at a consensus.
- A lot of people skipped this meeting. Expect surprises later.
- The business stakeholder has set everything to a high priority, without considering the burden it may pose on the team later.
- No consideration given to non-functional requirements such as security, performance, and usability, which could lead to future issues and tech debt. It's important to include them in the backlog now.

Here are some strategies to consider to make your refinement sessions better.

- **Regular Refinement Sessions**: Schedule dedicated time for Backlog Refinement in each sprint. This ensures that the backlog remains up-to-date and relevant.

- **Refine User Stories**: Work as a team to clarify user stories, add acceptance criteria, and ensure they are ready for sprint planning.
- **Break Down Tasks**: Identify large backlog items and break them down into smaller, manageable tasks. This will improve estimation and planning accuracy.
- **Estimate Tasks**: During refinement sessions, assign relative estimates to tasks. This helps you understand the effort required for each item.
- **Adjust Priorities**: Regularly review and adjust the priority of backlog items based on changing requirements, customer feedback, or business needs.

Make refinements a routine to always have two sprints worth of stories ready to work on. This way, the team will have enough work and the flow will be supported.

CHAPTER 4

Sprint Review / Demo

"The Demo Is Only for the Product Owner"

The Sprint Review is an essential element of the Agile framework, which allows the entire team to inspect the increment of work done during the sprint. It's a collaborative effort where the team and stakeholders can gather feedback and discuss the progress made during the sprint.

Contrary to popular misconception, the Sprint Review isn't just a presentation of the team's completed work to the Product Owner. Instead, it is an interactive and engaging session where the team showcases its accomplishments and gathers valuable stakeholder feedback.

During the review, the team and stakeholders discuss the work completed during the sprint, the challenges encountered, and the insights gained. Based on the feedback, the team can then adjust the backlog. This collaborative approach helps the team improve the product incrementally and deliver the best possible value to the stakeholders.

Sprint Review session is a crucial component of the Agile framework that promotes collaboration, transparency, and continuous improvement.

It has been a while since Matt and his team started the sprint. Let's check if they have any review sessions planned.

Matt: *Hey Don, our Sprint Review is coming up. Are you ready to demo our work?*

Don: *Yeah, I'll put together a presentation for the Product Owner. They're the main audience, right?*

Matt: *Well, yes, the Product Owner is a key stakeholder. But remember, the Sprint Review is for the whole team and stakeholders too.*

Don: *So, should I just run through the tasks completed and call it a day?*

Matt: *Not quite. It's not just about showing what we've done but also gathering feedback. It's a chance for stakeholders to see the product in action and give us their thoughts.*

Don: *Ah, got it. I guess it's more of a conversation than a one-way presentation.*

Matt: *Exactly. We want to engage stakeholders, answer their questions, and get their input on what we've built.*

Don: *What if they suggest changes or new features during the review?*

Matt: *That's the beauty of it! We can capture those suggestions, discuss their impact, and decide whether to include them in the backlog.*

✓ Watch your workplace	
Anti-Pattern Observed	Corrective Action
• A senior member is presenting their work and everyone else is watching.	This is not recommended. It is important to seek direct feedback from stakeholders by reviewing their work.
• Review sessions are being cancelled repeatedly, and it's worth noting that they are not mandatory.	Ensure these sessions occur even if work is incomplete. Detect issues early.
• The session is exclusively for the product owner, and no one else is invited.	Ideally, all stakeholders involved in the respective projects, including other teams developing dependent features, should be invited.

Invite the Whole Team: Encourage all team members to participate in the Sprint Review, not just those presenting.

Engage Stakeholders: Invite stakeholders to provide feedback, ask questions, and share their thoughts during the demo.

Demonstrate Working Features: Focus on showcasing working features or increments of the product, not just slides or plans.

Capture Feedback: Have a mechanism to capture feedback and suggestions during the review for later discussion.

Adjust Backlog: Based on the feedback received, discuss with the team and Product Owner to adjust the product backlog as needed.

Teams can use the Sprint Review to collect valuable insights, involve stakeholders, and confirm that the product is heading in the right direction. It is important to debunk the misconception that the Sprint Review is solely for the Product Owner, as the entire team can use this ceremony.

Review session happens once per Sprint duration. However, It is a great idea to have frequent demos of the work items to the product owners, business stakeholders or any interested parties involved so that the progress is measured then and there. Feedbacks are not necessarily to be worked on immediately, but can be captured in the backlog, discuss during the next refinement session and pull it into the sprint during the planning session. Please note, the Sprint Goal remains the same.

CHAPTER 5

Retrospective

"It's Just a Complaining Session"

Retrospective is one of the essential components of Agile. However, it is often misunderstood as a simple complaint session where team members express their frustrations without any clear purpose or direction. This misconception can lead to teams viewing retrospectives as unproductive and time-consuming meetings that yield little value. The Retrospective is a structured and intentional gathering of the team to reflect on the sprint, assess what worked well, identify areas for improvement, and collaboratively plan actionable steps to enhance future performance. The Retrospective aims to enable the team to learn from their mistakes and successes, identify any obstacles or inefficiencies that may have arisen during the sprint, and work together to address these issues.

The Retrospective allows the team to analyze their processes and identify any bottlenecks or gaps hindering their progress. By doing so, the team can make necessary adjustments and improve their workflows, leading to a more efficient and effective team delivering a high-quality product.

To achieve this, the Retrospective session should be well-structured and helped by a skilled Scrum Master or Agile

Coach. The team should be encouraged to discuss their thoughts and ideas openly, and the facilitator should guide the conversation toward actionable steps that the team can take to improve their processes.

There is no requirement for a specific format for this meeting, but there are many formats to choose from if you would like. The "Start, Stop, Continue" retrospective meeting format is a simple and effective way for teams practicing Agile methodologies, particularly Scrum, to reflect on their work and improve. Its purpose is to gather feedback from team members on what they should start, stop, and continue doing in future sprints to improve their processes and productivity.

Here's an explanation of each element of the "Start, Stop, Continue" format:

Start

During the "Start" phase of the retrospective, team members discuss and identify actions, practices, or processes that are not currently in place, but should be implemented in the upcoming sprint. These could be new ideas, processes, or approaches that the team believes will be beneficial and help them achieve their goals more efficiently.

Examples of "Start" items:

- Introducing pair programming for complex tasks.
- Conducting user testing earlier in Sprint.
- Setting aside time for knowledge-sharing sessions.

Stop

In the "Stop" section, team members discuss practices, behaviors, or actions that are not working well or are hindering the team's progress. They identify things that should be discontinued or eliminated to improve efficiency and effectiveness.

Examples of "Stop" items:

- Endless discussions in meetings without clear outcomes.
- Overloading sprints with too many tasks.
- Allowing scope creep without proper evaluation.

Continue

In the "Continue" section, the team takes a moment to reflect on the practices, processes, or behaviors currently working well and should be continued in the next sprint. These could be successful practices that contribute positively to the team's productivity and outcomes. This helps the team keep its momentum and build on its successes.

Examples of "Continue" items:

- Daily stand-up meetings for quick updates.
- Using a specific project management tool that has been effective.
- Regularly updating the team's Kanban board for visibility.

A sample screenshot of the start, stop, continue method is provided below. We can even capture notes using a text editor. If you prefer to use a more sophisticated tool, Confluence is a good possibility, and MIRO is an alternative tool you can consider.

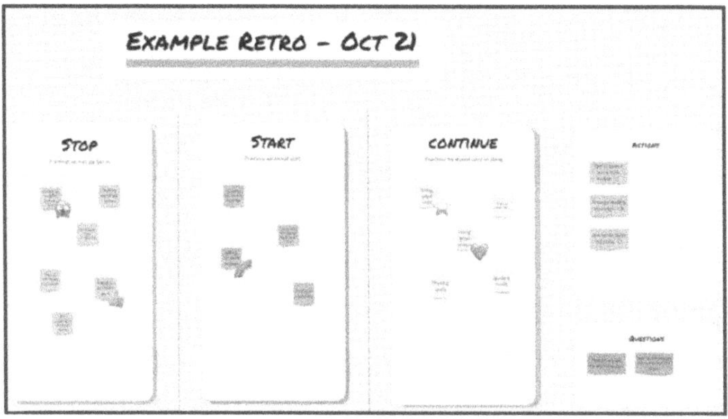

Fig 3: Sample Retro illustration using Start, Stop and Continue Method

How It Works:

- **Gather Feedback:** The Scrum Master or facilitator asks team members to individually write their "Start, Stop, Continue" ideas on sticky notes or a shared digital board.
- **Grouping Ideas:** After everyone has written their ideas, related items are grouped to find common themes or trends.
- **Discussion:** The team discusses each grouped item, focusing on understanding the reasons behind the suggestions and their potential impact.
- **Action Items:** From these discussions, the team finds actionable items for improvement, assigns ownership, and sets specific goals or changes for the next sprint.

Instead of using the Start, Stop, continue method, we can implement the What Went Well, What Went Wrong, and Areas of Improvement approach. This method is similar but takes a different approach to finding what worked well and what didn't and collecting any suggestions for improvement from the team. Note that the retro session can be moderated by Scrum Masters or someone within the team who can also do it.

Visual artifacts are captivating, and the Sailboat Retro format makes retro sessions more engaging and enjoyable. The "Sailboat Retrospective" is an alternative and creative format that uses a sailboat metaphor to visualize the team's journey, obstacles, and elements that propel them forward. It's a fun and engaging way to gather feedback and insights from team members.

Here's an explanation of the Sailboat Retrospective format:

Setup:

- **Draw a Sailboat:** The facilitator draws a simple sailboat illustration on paper or whiteboard. The boat represents the team's project or journey.
- **Add Elements:**

- **Islands (Positive Aspects):** Draw islands around the sailboat, representing positive aspects or achievements. These could be things the team did well, accomplishments, or positive experiences.
- **Anchors (Obstacles):** Draw anchors beneath the sailboat, symbolizing obstacles or challenges that slowed down progress or hindered the team.
- **Wind (Helpful Factors):** Draw wind or gusts blowing into the boat's sails, representing factors that helped the team move forward or achieve success.
- **Icebergs (Potential Risks):** Optionally, draw icebergs in the water, symbolizing potential risks or threats that the team needs to be aware of.

Fig 4: Sailboat Retro illustration

How It Works:

- **Gather Input:** Team members are given time to write down their thoughts on sticky notes individually.
  - Positive Aspects (Islands): Things that went well, achievements, successful practices, or positive experiences.
  - Obstacles (Anchors): Challenges, blockers, issues, or anything that slowed down progress.
  - Helpful Factors (Wind): Factors that helped the team, such as new tools, improved communication, or collaboration.
  - Risks (Icebergs): The team should be mindful of potential risks or threats in upcoming sprints.

- **Place on the Sailboat:**
    - Each team member places their sticky notes on the corresponding parts of the sailboat:
    - Positive Aspects (Islands) on the islands around the sailboat.
    - Obstacles (Anchors) under the sailboat as anchors.
    - Helpful Factors (Wind) on the sail indicate what's propelling the boat forward.
    - Risks (Icebergs), if included, can be placed in the water around the sailboat.
- **Discussion:**
    - The team discusses each element on the sailboat, focusing on understanding the reasons behind them.
    - For positive aspects (islands) and helpful factors (wind), the team can discuss how to keep and use these in future sprints.
    - For obstacles (anchors) and risks (icebergs), the team brainstorms solutions, mitigation strategies, or action items to address these in the next iteration.
- **Action Items:**
    - The team finds actionable items from the discussions and assigns owners to follow up on them in the upcoming sprint.

Benefits:

Visual Representation: The sailboat metaphor provides a visual representation of the team's journey, making it easier to find strengths, weaknesses, and potential risks.

Engagement: It encourages team members to actively participate by visualizing their feedback on the sailboat.

Holistic View: By examining positive aspects, obstacles, and helpful factors together, the team gains a holistic view of its performance.

Creativity and Fun: The metaphorical approach adds an element of creativity and fun to the retrospective, making it more engaging for team members.

It's important to hold a retrospective after every sprint, no matter what method is used. If you have a four-week sprint and think a retrospective is necessary every two weeks, schedule one. Remember that timely feedback is a fundamental aspect of the agile method, and retrospective sessions are a wonderful way to gain insight into team collaboration. Using these sessions, you can bring your team closer together and strive for continuous improvement.

- **Focus on Solutions, Not Just Problems**:
  - Encourage team members to move beyond surface-level complaints and delve into the root causes of issues.
  - Retro sessions will reveal the underlying problems when people are transparent, but what happens when you have an issue found? Use techniques like the "5 Whys" to uncover deeper insights into problems and find solutions.
- **Celebrate Successes and Wins**:
  - Allocate time during the Retrospective to acknowledge achievements, no matter how small.
  - Research shows that teams with a culture of celebration and recognition often have higher levels of engagement and performance.
- **Actionable Items with Ownership**:
  - For each identified improvement, assign specific action items with clear owners and deadlines.
  - This ensures accountability and follow-through on proposed solutions.
- **Continuous Monitoring and Follow-Up**:
  - Review action items from earlier retrospectives to track progress and evaluate their impact.

- Adjust future retrospective discussions based on the outcomes of earlier action items.

✓ Watch your workplace

- A person raises an issue, which everyone acknowledges, but others hesitate to voice their own concerns.
- Fear or lack of confidence prevents individuals from bringing prominent issues to light.
- Action items found in earlier sessions are often overlooked or not followed through.
- Retro sessions are often ignored by many or are consistently cancelled.
- There is little to no enthusiasm for recognizing and celebrating the successes and achievements of the Sprint.

When any of the symptoms mentioned above surface within your organization, it is crucial to take them seriously. While there might be several reasons behind these occurrences, addressing the obvious ones is important to instill confidence in the team about the process. For instance, if previously identified action items show no progress, it's natural for the team to lose interest in sharing further concerns, seeing little hope for resolution. Similarly, a lack of enthusiasm from the team could indicate a depreciation in motivation, requiring immediate attention from management.

The leadership team must not be invited to the retro meetings. A big No to them, only for this meeting, though.

It is recommended that management stakeholders not be invited to the retrospective meetings. Team members might hesitate to voice their genuine concerns out of fear, especially if management representatives are present. Additionally, having management in the meeting might lead to immediate attempts to answer or justify the raised issues. This can inadvertently diminish the importance of the meeting and the value of open, candid discussions.

Instead, the retrospective should serve as a safe space for the team to freely express their thoughts without concern for immediate resolution or justification. This environment encourages honest feedback, enabling the team to check the root causes of issues and collaboratively develop actionable solutions. By keeping management out of the meeting, team members are more likely to openly discuss challenges, successes, and areas for improvement, leading to more meaningful outcomes from the retrospective process.

It's important to note that retrospectives aren't limited to issues within the process or project management alone. They can also be used to address everyday office matters that may affect productivity. For instance, something seemingly minor, like inadequate-quality snacks in the office cafeteria, could prompt employees to seek breaks elsewhere, reducing overall productivity. Therefore, it's essential not to underestimate the significance of such issues, as their effects might be more substantial than initially perceived.

CHAPTER 6

WIP Limits (Kanban)

"More Tasks in Progress Means Faster Completion"

Kanban methodology is a popular approach for managing work items efficiently and streamlined. One of its foundational concepts is work-in-progress (WIP) limits. These limits restrict the number of tasks being worked on at any given time, leading to improved flow efficiency and reduced delays.

Picture a Kanban board, a visual symphony of columns being the stages of work, from "To Do" to "Done." Each column, a stage in the value production, holds a finite number of tasks carefully curated by the WIP limit. This limit, a delicate dance of constraint and liberation, dictates the maximum number of tasks allowed in each column at any given moment.

One might ponder why this constraint exists. Optimizing flow is the heart of Kanban's philosophy. By limiting the number of tasks in progress, teams can prevent the cacophony of multitasking and task overload. This intentional constraint fosters focus, enabling team members to devote their undivided attention to several tasks, ensuring each receives the time and energy it deserves.

Consider a team with a WIP limit of 3 tasks for the "In Progress" column. As one task moves to completion, a new task is pulled into the column, keeping the delicate balance of work. Should a team member meet a roadblock, the WIP limit serves as a safety net, preventing the accumulation of stagnant tasks and encouraging swift collaboration to resolve the obstacle.

Yet, the beauty of WIP limits extends beyond the tangible realm of task management. They catalyze continuous improvement, a recurring motif in the Kanban melody. As teams see the effects of their WIP limits—spotting bottlenecks, finding inefficiencies—they are prompted to refine and recalibrate, fine-tuning their process with each iteration.

In this Kanban symphony, WIP limits appear as the conductor's baton, guiding teams toward a harmonious work rhythm. They instill discipline, foster focus, and illuminate the path to flow. With each task pulled into the board and each WIP limit carefully set, teams orchestrate a symphony of efficiency, productivity, and continuous improvement, creating a masterpiece of agile success.

Despite this, many teams mistakenly believe that by starting and working on more tasks simultaneously, they can speed up the completion of work. However, the truth is that this leads to overcrowded boards and tasks piling up, causing bottlenecks, delays, and reduced throughput. WIP limits are a crucial element in Kanban methodology, as they help to perfect flow and minimize the time it takes for work items to move from start to finish. By restricting the number of tasks in progress at any given time, teams can focus on completing work before moving on to the next. This helps to reduce multitasking and improve overall throughput, resulting in faster delivery times and improved customer satisfaction. When the number of tasks in progress is limited, the team can better understand the capacity of their workflow and how it can be improved.

Matt found a lot of in-progress items with Don and a few other members of the team. He wanted to check this with Don and coach him if he feels his understanding is not in line with the best practices of Agile. Let's listen...

Matt: *Hey Don, I've noticed our Kanban board is jam-packed with tasks in progress. Are we trying to speed things up by working on everything at once?*

Don: *Yeah, I figured the more tasks we have going, the faster we'll get things done. Isn't that the whole point?*

Matt: *It might seem that way, but in Kanban, it's all about optimizing flow. When we have too many tasks in progress, it can actually slow us down. You are aware of context-switching that leads to wastages, aren't you?*

Don: *Really? But won't limiting our work in progress just create bottlenecks?*

Matt: *Not if we do it right. WIP limits are there to help us maintain a steady flow of work. By focusing on completing tasks before starting new ones, we reduce context switching and improve efficiency.*

Don: *I see your point. So, how do we determine our WIP limits?*

Matt: *It's a bit of trial and error. We can start by analyzing our past performance and understanding our team's capacity.*

- *We should also consider the size and complexity of tasks, as well as any dependencies.*
- *The goal is to find a balance where we're not overwhelmed but still have enough work to keep us moving.*

Don: *Alright, let's try it. I'm all for improving our flow and efficiency. Thank you, Matt.*

When setting up limits for each column, you may wonder whether it should be based on the number of people or a random call. However, there is no fixed rule for this, and it is best to experiment until you find what works best for your team. Here are some pointers that may help you understand it better:

- **Analyzing Past Performance**:
    - Review historical data to understand the team's average completion rate and cycle times.
    - Use this information as a basis for setting initial WIP limits.
- **Consider Task Size and Complexity**:
    - Smaller, more manageable tasks generally flow through the system faster.
    - Adjust WIP limits based on the size and complexity of tasks to keep a steady flow.
- **Team Capacity and Dependencies**:
    - Consider the team's capacity to handle tasks effectively.
    - Consider dependencies between tasks and adjust WIP limits accordingly to prevent bottlenecks.
- **Gradual Adjustment and Experimentation**:

  - Start with conservative WIP limits and gradually adjust based on team feedback and observations.
  - Use cycle time and lead time metrics to assess the impact of WIP limits on flow efficiency.
- **Visualize Work and Limit WIP Violations**:
  - Use the Kanban board to visualize work items and track their progress.
  - Highlight WIP limit violations to make them visible and encourage the team to address them promptly.
- **Encourage Collaboration and Swarming**:
  - When a team member completes a task, encourage them to help others finish it instead of pulling another work in their bucket.
  - This promotes collaboration, reduces bottlenecks, and improves overall flow.
- **Regular Review and Reflection**:
  - Regular retrospectives should be conducted to reflect on the impact of WIP limits.
  - Gather feedback from the team on whether the current limits are effective or need adjustment.

Modern tools like JIRA have made implementing Work In Progress (WIP) limits effortless and effective. Below is a screenshot illustrating how to configure a Kanban board with minimum and maximum limits for the number of issues allowed in each column at any given time.

Fig 5: JIRA Kanban board with WIP limit configuration

> The best choice for the WIP limit is to set it at 2. This allows team members to focus on a task while having an alternative ready in case of any impediments. It's recommended not to surpass this limit unless there's a compelling reason to do so, ensuring smooth workflow and task management efficiency.

CHAPTER 7

Task Estimation

"Aiming for perfect estimation"

The art of estimation is a collaborative and iterative process that aims to bring clarity and predictability to project timelines. Traditional methods rely on fixed time limits, Agile estimation embraces a more dynamic and team-oriented approach, allowing for flexibility and adaptation in the face of evolving requirements. Story points are central to the Agile estimation process. They are a unit of measurement that captures the size relative to other work product and complexity of user stories or tasks. Instead of assigning precise time durations, teams use story points to gauge the effort and scope of each item concerning others.

Consider a scenario where a team begins their estimation journey with a simple story, "Create Login Page." They collectively assign this story a baseline of 5 story points. This establishes a reference point from which they can estimate other stories. For instance, if "User Registration" feels twice as complex as "Create Login Page," it might be assigned 10 story points. During a Planning Poker session, team members collectively estimate the story points for each task or user story. Each team member will be given a deck of cards representing different story point values (Ex., 1, 2, 3, 5, 8, etc.). As the team discusses and clarifies the details of a user story, each member privately selects a card representing their estimate of the story's complexity. Once everyone has chosen, the cards are revealed simultaneously. Any discrepancies in estimates prompt discussions, allowing team members to share insights, perspectives, and potential risks. This iterative discussion and recalibration process shows a consensus, refining the estimation accuracy.

With each sprint, the team gains a clearer understanding of their capacity and pace through velocity. Velocity is the average number of stories points the team completes in a sprint. Over time, this metric becomes a reliable indicator of the team's productivity and serves as a guiding light for future estimations. For instance, if the team consistently completes 30 story points in a two-week sprint, they can reasonably estimate that a backlog of 60 story points will take approximately two sprints to complete. This predictive power of velocity allows teams to plan and forecast project timelines with greater confidence and accuracy.

Task estimation is a critical aspect of Agile methodologies, providing teams with a basis for planning, prioritization, and resource allocation. However, a common misconception among teams is the belief that every task must be estimated with pinpoint accuracy, down to the last hour or minute. This myth can lead to excessive time spent on estimation, analysis paralysis, and a sense of failure when estimates don't align perfectly with actual results. Agile embraces the idea of "good enough" estimation, recognizing that perfection is unattainable and unnecessary for effective planning and delivery.

Matt: *Hey Don, I've noticed we're spending a lot of time trying to estimate every task down to the last detail. Do you think we're being too meticulous?*

Don: *Maybe a bit, but isn't it important to get our estimates right? We don't want to end up overcommitting or falling behind schedule.*

Matt: *Absolutely, but Agile isn't about perfection in estimates. It's about making informed decisions with the information we have.*

- *Overanalyzing and trying to estimate every task perfectly can lead to delays and missed opportunities.*

Don: *That makes sense, but how do we know if our estimates are good enough?*

Matt: *We aim for accurate estimates within a reasonable margin of error. It's about finding the balance between spending too much time on estimation and having a general idea of how long tasks will take.*

- *Remember, estimates are just that—estimates. They're not guarantees.*

Don: *So, how do we strike that balance?*

Matt: *Let's focus on relative estimation techniques like Planning Poker or T-Shirt Sizing.*

- *This helps us quickly estimate tasks based on their relative size and complexity compared to others.*
- *We also need to revisit and adjust our estimates as we gather more information throughout the project.*

Don: *Alright, I see what you're saying. Let's aim for good enough estimates and adjust as needed.*

- **Relative Estimation Techniques**:
    - Use techniques like Planning Poker / T-shirt sizing to quickly estimate the work product based on their relative size and complexity.

  - Using Story Point units encourages collaboration among team members and reduces the need for precise hour-based estimates.
- **Focus on Range Estimates**:
  - Instead of providing a single-point estimate, offer a range that accounts for potential variability.
  - For example, "This task is estimated to be between 2 to 4 Story Points." But when you record, you may strike an average estimate it requires.
- **Use Historical Data and Trends**:
  - Refer to past project data to inform current estimations.
  - Identify patterns and trends in task completion times to guide future estimates.
- **Embrace the Cone of Uncertainty**:
  - Understand that estimates become more accurate as more information becomes available.
  - Communicate to stakeholders that early estimates have a wider margin of error that narrows as the project progresses.

- **Regularly Review and Adjust Estimates**:
    - Conduct regular backlog Refinement sessions to revisit and refine task estimates.
    - Adjust estimates based on the latest information, team feedback, or changing project requirements.
- **Encourage Collaboration and Consensus**:
    - Involve the entire team in estimation sessions to use collective knowledge and perspectives.
    - This promotes shared understanding and ownership of the estimates.
- **Focus on Value Delivery**:
    - Ultimately, the goal is to deliver value to the customer.
    - Prioritize tasks on their impact and value and rather than solely on estimated time.

✓ Watch your workplace

↷ Only a few people, such as technical leads or architects, provide estimates, while others stay calm.

↷ Missed deadlines are often blamed by management, which can affect estimates. To compensate, people tend to add increased buffers.

- Time estimates are currently used instead of story point estimates. While this is a good starting point, it's important to eventually transition to story point estimates.
- Consistent differences between planned and actual estimates can show a lack of corrective measures, ongoing impediments, management pressure, or other types of failures. It's important to watch this closely and take proper action to resolve the issues.

The journey of Agile estimation is a continuous process of improvement and refinement rather than a static one. As teams progress through sprints, they gather valuable insights into their estimation practices, discovering areas where they have overestimated, underestimated, or met uncertainties. Teams reflect on their past estimations and find patterns during regular retrospectives and review sessions. They adjust their approach accordingly, refining their definition of story points, recalibrating their Planning Poker sessions, or introducing new techniques to enhance the accuracy of their estimations.

The estimation process is like a compass in the vast ocean of Agile project management, guiding teams toward project success. Agile teams navigate the seas of uncertainty with confidence and agility by embracing the language of story points, the collaborative spirit of Planning Poker, and the guiding light of team velocity. Teams unlock the power of Agile estimation by committing to open communication and continuous refinement. They turn uncertainties into actionable insights and complex tasks into achievable milestones.

Good scrum master keeps record of past incidents and remind teams during the refinement sessions to bring out better estimates. Ask questions, remind potential blockers, dependencies with other components and point out if the estimate seems unreasonable. Also, use physical deck of cards and make it like a play session so the team involvement gets better. Bottomline is to bring everyone to attend to the session and make them contribute.

CHAPTER 8

Role Misconceptions

"The Scrum Master Is a Project Manager"

One of the most common misconceptions people have about Agile is that the role of the Scrum Master is the same as that of a traditional Project Manager. Although there are some similarities in helping the teams and removing impediments, it's important to understand that the responsibilities and focus of these roles are fundamentally different. This confusion often arises from personal understanding versus organizational culture. When project managers with authority over resources start to adopt agile, it can be challenging to give up the traditional mindset and embrace it.

Roles of a Project Manager

Project Managers work within the five phases and ten knowledge areas defined by the PMBOK (Project Management Body of Knowledge by PMI), a widely recognized project management standard. However, a project manager must focus on certain areas, such as planning and scheduling, resource management, risk management, and stakeholder communication.

Planning and scheduling are the important tasks of a Project Manager's role. They lay the groundwork for the project by developing detailed plans, defining milestones, and creating schedules. This helps ensure the project is executed well enough to get everyone involved and bring them on the same page.

Resource management is another important responsibility of a Project Manager. They distribute resources, such as human capital, budgetary allocations, or materials, to ensure the project runs efficiently and effectively. This involves managing and distributing resources to meet project goals and timelines.

Risk management is another area in which project managers excel. They find potential risks, develop mitigation strategies, and watch risk factors throughout the project lifecycle. This helps ensure that risks are minimized and that the project is delivered on time and within budget.

Stakeholder Communication is a key responsibility of a Project Manager. They serve as the primary point of contact for stakeholders, providing updates, addressing concerns, and managing expectations. Effective communication is essential to ensure everyone works towards the same goal and that the project is delivered successfully.

Roles of a Scrum Master

At the heart of Agile methodology stands the Scrum Master—a facilitator, coach, and guardian of Agile values. Their primary focus lies in fostering the Agile mindset within the team, ensuring adherence to Scrum practices, and removing impediments that hinder progress.

Facilitating Scrum events: From sprint planning to daily stand-ups and retrospectives, the Scrum Master orchestrates these ceremonies, ensuring they run smoothly and efficiently.

Shielding the team: They act as a shield, protecting the team from external distractions and impediments, allowing them to focus on delivering value.

Coaching and mentoring: The Scrum Master nurtures a culture of continuous improvement, guiding the team towards self-organization and effective collaboration.

Removing impediments: Whether resolving conflicts, addressing resource constraints, or clearing roadblocks, the Scrum Master ensures nothing obstructs the team's progress.

Matt: *Hey Don, I think there's a bit of confusion about what the Scrum Master's role really entails. Some team members seem to think they're just like Project Managers.*

Don: *I've noticed that too. I think it's because the titles sound similar, but their roles are quite different in Agile.*

Matt: *Exactly, Don. The Scrum Master isn't here to manage the project but to serve the team and assure the effectiveness of the team within the Scrum framework.*

They focus on removing impediments, facilitating meetings, and helping the team understand and embrace Agile principles.

Don: *So, they're more of a coach and facilitator than a manager?*

Matt: *That's a good way to put it. They coach the team on Agile practices, facilitate Scrum ceremonies like Daily Stand-ups and Retrospectives, and shield the team from external distractions.*

Don: *That makes sense. I guess we need to clarify these roles to avoid confusion.*

Matt: *Absolutely. When team members understand the distinct roles of the Scrum Master and Project Manager, it helps create a more effective and collaborative environment.*

Don: *Can we not create a RACI kind of document and publish it so everyone in alignment?*

Matt: *I wouldn't recommend that, Don. It takes us back to traditional project management mode. Agile is about shifting culture and respecting change. This should come through learning and cultural changes. Therefore, it is ideal to coach everyone to achieve this.*

Aspect	Scrum Master	Project Manager
Methodology	Agile (Scrum/kanban/etc.)	Traditional (Waterfall/V-Model, etc.)
Focus	Team facilitation, Agile principles	Project planning, execution, monitoring
Responsibilities	Shielding team, removing impediments	Planning, resource management, risk mitigation
Ceremonies	Facilitates Scrum events	Develops project plans, schedules
Scope	Primarily team-centric	Broader project-centric approach
Flexibility	Embraces change, adapts quickly	Adheres to predefined plans, milestones

Here are some ideas you may use to avoid this misunderstanding.

- **Educate on Scrum Master Responsibilities**:
    - Communicate the role of the Scrum Master as a servant-leader for the team.
    - Emphasize their responsibilities in facilitating Agile practices, removing impediments, and

promoting a culture of continuous improvement.

- **Differentiate from Project Manager Role**:
    - Provide clarity on the differences between a Scrum Master and a traditional Project Manager.
    - Highlight that while a Project Manager may focus on project plans and schedules, the Scrum Master empowers the team to deliver value.
- **Promote Servant-Leadership**:
    - Encourage the Scrum Master to adopt a servant-leadership mindset, prioritizing the team's needs above theirs.
    - This includes facilitating team discussions, helping to resolve conflicts, and promoting self-organization.
- **Facilitate Agile Practices**:
    - Ensure the Scrum Master has the resources and support to facilitate Scrum ceremonies effectively.
    - This includes organizing and leading Daily Stand-ups, Sprint Planning, Reviews, and Retrospectives.

- **Empower the Team**:
    - Encourage the Scrum Master to empower the team to take ownership of their work and decisions.
    - Foster a culture of self-organization, where the team collaboratively plans and executes tasks.
- **Provide Continuous Training and Support**:
    - Offer training sessions or workshops on Agile principles and Scrum practices.
    - Provide ongoing support and mentorship to help the Scrum Master grow in their role.
- **Clarify Expectations with Stakeholders**:
    - Communicate to stakeholders the role of the Scrum Master in facilitating team effectiveness and Agile practices.
    - Set expectations that Scrum Master is a servant leader and they are different from Project Managers.

In the transformative journey towards Agile methodologies, a critical juncture appears when the roles of the Scrum Master and the Project Manager are clarified. This pivotal moment holds the potential to shape the trajectory of Agile adoption within the organization, ensuring a solid foundation for success. Central to this clarity is the role of the leadership team—the vanguards of change and champions of Agile principles. It falls upon the leadership team to define and articulate the distinct roles of the Scrum Master and the Project Manager. By clearly delineating each role's responsibilities, expectations, and nuances, the leadership team sets the stage for a harmonious collaboration between Agile practices and traditional project management.

During this transformation, the Scrum Master appears as a beacon of Agile principles—a facilitator, coach, and guardian of the Agile mindset. However, to fully embody this role and confidently guide the team towards Agile excellence, the Scrum Master needs unwavering support from the leadership team and sponsors.

Dispelling the myth that the Scrum Master is merely a stand-in for the Project Manager needs a concerted effort from organizational leaders. It is not enough to assign the title of Scrum Master; true empowerment comes from a deep understanding and endorsement of the role's significance. When the leadership team stands firmly behind the Scrum Master, offering guidance, resources, and unwavering support, a transformative shift occurs. The Scrum Master is no longer seen as a secondary figure but as a pivotal force driving the Agile transformation forward.

With this support, the Scrum Master gains the confidence to coach the team effectively, navigate challenges with agility, and foster a culture of continuous improvement. The organization reaps the benefits of Agile methodologies—enhanced collaboration, adaptability to change, and accelerated value delivery.

> In many organizations, the role of the scrum master often fails due to various factors such as confusion surrounding their responsibilities, lack of support from leadership, and insufficient training. The presence of the scrum master is sometimes questioned and perceived as unnecessary. However, the scrum master is a crucial role in any organization that implements Agile methodology. They are responsible for ensuring that the process runs smoothly, and if they fail, the organization as a whole suffers. Unfortunately, scrum masters often fail because they are not given the opportunity to perform their duties effectively.

CHAPTER 9

Overlooking Technical Debt

"We'll Deal with Technical Debt Later"

It's a common misconception among teams to postpone addressing technical debt, believing they can "deal with it later" after delivering initial features or meeting deadlines.

However, delaying the resolution of technical debt can lead to compounding issues over time. The codebase becomes more complicated to maintain, bugs increase, and the team's velocity slows down as they spend more time fixing problems rather than delivering new features. Ultimately, the cost of addressing technical debt later often outweighs the benefits of quick gains in the short term.

It's essential to manage technical debt effectively to ensure the success of software projects. Technical debt describes the consequences of prioritizing new features over code refactoring. When developers make frequent changes to the code without thorough refactoring, it leads to code complexity and duplication, which further adds to technical debt. If not checked, technical debt can manifest in detrimental ways to the project's success. Unchecked technical debt can increase bug counts, longer debugging cycles, and decreased code maintainability. These issues can lead to missed deadlines, unhappy stakeholders, and a loss of confidence in the product's reliability. It's crucial to address technical debt proactively and strategically to prevent these issues from occurring.

Developers and stakeholders need to take a proactive approach to addressing technical debts. Consider allocating a portion of each sprint to code refactoring, documentation improvement, and test coverage enhancement. By dedicating time and resources to these tasks, teams can prevent tech debt accumulation and ensure the codebase remains clean and maintainable.

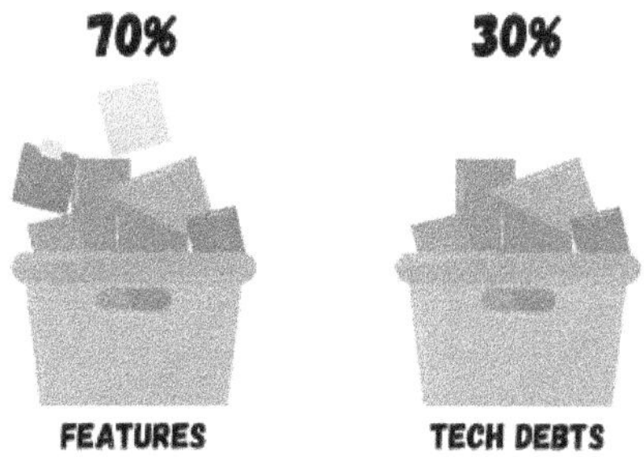

Fig 6: Features and Tech Debt Backlogs

Another approach is to create a prioritized list of technical debt items alongside the product backlog, known as the "Tech Debt Backlog." During sprint planning, teams can select several items from the tech debt backlog to address alongside new feature development. This approach ensures teams focus on new features and code quality, preventing technical debt from accumulating.

Some organizations opt for dedicated "Hardening Sprints" to tackle accumulated technical debt. These sprints, typically at the end of a development cycle, focus solely on addressing technical issues, improving code quality, and conducting thorough testing. While hardening sprints can be effective, they often indicate a reactive rather than proactive approach to technical debt. Ideally, teams should integrate technical debt management into their regular sprint cycles, ensuring a balanced focus on new features and code quality. Managing technical debt effectively is crucial for the success of any software project. To prevent the accumulation of technical debt and ensure that the codebase remains clean and maintainable, teams can take a proactive approach by implementing strategies such as allocating time for code refactoring, creating a backlog for tech debt, and integrating technical debt management into regular sprint cycles. These measures will help teams keep their codebase in good shape and avoid the negative consequences of technical debt.

Matt: *Don, I've been observing the technical debt we've been accumulating lately. Rushing for deadlines leaves us with messy code and potential risks down the line.*

Don: *It's definitely a challenge. Balancing speed and code quality is crucial. Could you elaborate on what you've been noticing specifically?*

Matt: *Last sprint, we had to skip writing unit tests for a critical feature to meet the deadline. Now, every change feels risky without those tests in place.*

Don: *I see what you mean. We've encountered similar situations before, especially with the need to refactor quickly for new requirements.*

Matt: *Exactly. We must address this technical debt before it becomes a significant burden. I propose allocating some bandwidth in each sprint for technical debt tasks alongside our feature work.*

Don: *That sounds like a good plan. How would we go about prioritizing these tasks?*

Matt: *We can create a tech debt backlog similar to our product backlog. This will help us keep track of these tasks, prioritize them, and plan them into our sprints.*

Don: *Ah, that makes sense. It ensures we're not just focusing on new features but also on maintaining a healthy codebase.*

Matt: *Absolutely. Additionally, I've heard of teams using hardening sprints to tackle accumulated technical debt. However, it's more effective to integrate tech debt tasks into our regular sprints.*

Don: *Could you elaborate on that? Why integrate them instead of having dedicated hardening sprints?*

Matt: *Certainly. Hardening sprints can sometimes indicate a reactive approach to technical debt. Ideally, we want to handle it as we go, alongside our feature development.*

Don: *I see your point. So, by allocating time for tech debt tasks in each sprint, we're addressing issues proactively rather than waiting for them to accumulate.*

Matt: *Exactly, Don. It's about balancing delivering new features and maintaining a healthy codebase. Small, regular efforts to address tech debt prevent the need for large cleanup efforts later on.*

Don: *I appreciate the clarity, Matt. It makes sense to tackle these issues as part of our regular process rather than treating them as separate tasks.*

Matt: *Absolutely, Don. It's all about continuous improvement and ensuring the long-term success of our projects. I'll bring up the idea of allocating time for tech debt tasks in our upcoming planning session.*

Don: *Thank you, Matt. I see the value of this approach and will benefit our team greatly.*

To successfully manage tech debts, we can follow the following practices. We trust that agile provides values and principles, so we can enhance our working methods without breaking these fundamentals.

- **Identify and Prioritize Technical Debt**:
    - Conduct regular code reviews and analyses to identify areas of the codebase with high technical debt.
    - Prioritize these items alongside new features in the backlog to ensure they are addressed promptly.
- **Incremental Refactoring and Improvement**:
    - Break down large technical debt items into smaller, manageable tasks.
    - Address technical debt incrementally with each sprint, dedicating a portion of the team's

capacity to refactoring and improving code quality.

- **Automated Testing and Quality Assurance**:
    - Implement automated testing frameworks to catch regressions and prevent new technical debt from accumulating.
    - Invest time in creating a suite of tests covering critical codebase areas.
- **Allocate Time for Refactoring**:
    - Reserve time in each sprint specifically for refactoring and addressing technical debt.
    - This ensures that technical debt is not continually pushed aside in favor of new features.
- **Code Reviews and Pair Programming**:
    - Encourage regular code reviews to catch potential technical debt early.
    - Pair programming can also help improve code quality and reduce the likelihood of introducing new debt.
- **Educate the Team on the Importance of Technical Debt**:
    - Help the team understand the long-term consequences of accumulating technical debt.

    - Foster a culture that values code quality, maintainability, and long-term project health.
- **Use Metrics to Track Technical Debt**:
    - Implement metrics such as code complexity, code churn, and bug counts to track the impact of technical debt over time.
    - Use these metrics to make data-driven decisions on prioritizing and addressing technical debt.

Effective technical debt management is not merely a matter of writing better code; it is a strategic investment in the long-term success of software projects. By recognizing its presence, understanding its implications, and implementing proactive measures, teams can navigate the complexities of software development with agility, efficiency, and confidence.

CHAPTER 10

Adapting Agile to the Organization

"Agile Is One-Size-Fits-All"

Agile methodology has significantly transformed project and product management with its 4 manifesto values and 12 principles. These values and principles have laid a strong foundation for teams to adopt iterative development, customer collaboration, and responsiveness to change. However, there is a common misconception that Agile is a rigid, one-size-fits-all philosophy. In reality, Agile is all about flexibility and adaptability. It provides a set of guiding principles, but the frameworks built upon these principles can—and should—be customized to meet each team or organization's specific needs and context.

Agile's core values and principles provide a strong foundation for teams to build upon. By customizing the frameworks to meet each team or organization's specific needs and context, teams can achieve their goals more effectively and efficiently.

Agile frameworks such as Scrum, Kanban, and Extreme Programming (XP) are widely used in software development companies to improve project management and increase productivity. Many people misunderstand these frameworks despite their benefits, viewing them as strict rules rather than flexible tools. It is important to remember that these frameworks are only meant to provide guidance and structure to Agile teams. To clarify, Agile frameworks are designed to be adapted and customized to fit each project or organization's unique needs and circumstances. For instance, a small co-located team may find that the daily stand-up meetings prescribed by Scrum are too formal and rigid for their needs. In this case, they may choose to have more informal check-ins instead while still following the core principles of transparency and communication. You may note that Scrum Guide 2020 removed this prescriptive format to facilitate this customization to a greater level. Similarly, a large enterprise with complex dependencies may find that the time-boxed sprints of Scrum do not align with their workflow. In such cases, they may opt for a Kanban approach that allows for continuous flow while still upholding Agile values of customer focus and responsiveness to change.

The key takeaway here is to view Agile frameworks as flexible tools that can be tailored to facilitate the unique needs of projects or organization. By doing so, teams can reap the benefits of Agile methodologies while avoiding the misconception of rigid rules that do not fit their needs.

The successful Agile implementation happens when we understand the values and principles behind it and then tailoring the frameworks accordingly. Here are some ways teams can customize Agile to fit their needs:

Tailoring Process and Tool: Agile methodology promotes iterative experimentation and learning from mistakes. It allows teams to modify their processes, try new approaches, and adapt based on feedback. To benefit from this, it is important to use retrospective sessions effectively to collect developer feedback and customize the process and tools to support the process customizations. For example, JIRA's out-of-the-box reports may not provide sufficient information for the leadership team. In such cases, you have the freedom to tailor the process, force the team to follow the steps to gather the required data and modify the tool to generate reports that meet your needs.

Empowered Teams: Agile methodology has eliminated the centralized decision-making power and has empowered every role to make decisions. This approach ensures that every voice counts and everyone feels their presence. If something doesn't work out as intended, anyone on the team can suggest a change at any point in time. The best place to raise such suggestions is during a retrospective session.

Adaptable workflows: Agile frameworks provide a great starting point for workflows, but it's important to remember that these workflows should be adaptable. As the project progresses, teams should be able to add or remove steps, adjust ceremonies, and experiment with new techniques. Teams can enjoy various customizations by implementing these workflows in tools like JIRA. For example, if you want to require certain data gathering for a specific workflow state, it's very possible and in line with agile principles. That being said, ensuring that the data being gathered aligns with the team's values and that everyone feels safe and happy in the process is crucial.

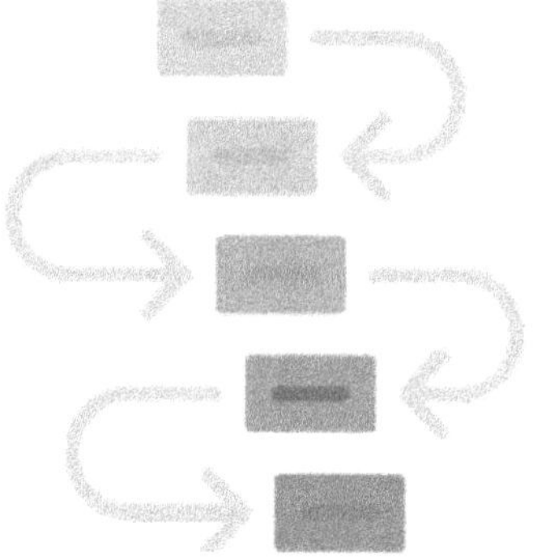

Matt: *Hey Don, we need to talk about how we're implementing Agile in our organization. It feels like we're trying to fit a square peg into a round hole.*

Don: *I know what you mean. It's like we're following Agile practices by the book without considering whether they really fit our team and projects.*

Matt: *Exactly, Don. Agile isn't meant to be a one-size-fits-all solution. It's about adapting and evolving to meet our organization's unique needs and challenges.*

- *We need to consider our team's dynamics, project requirements, and organizational culture when implementing Agile practices.*

Don: *But how do we know what aspects of Agile to keep and what to modify?*

Matt: *That's a good question. We can start by thoroughly assessing our current processes, identifying pain points, and understanding where Agile practices can add value.*

- *From there, we can selectively choose Agile principles and practices that align with our goals and adapt them to fit our context.*

Don: *So, Agile is more of a framework we can tailor to our needs rather than a strict set of rules?*

Matt: *Exactly, Don. Agile provides guiding principles and values that we can use as a foundation.*

- *It's about finding the balance between structure and flexibility so we can continuously improve and adapt our processes.*

Don: *I see what you mean. Let's ensure we're not just following Agile blindly but customizing it to suit our organization's needs.*

Agile coaches and trained agile implementation consultants play a critical role in organizations' initial stages of agile adoption. They conduct a thorough assessment of the system, leadership, and organizational needs and, based on the assessment, set up a process that best meets the organization's specific goals.

- **Assessment and Analysis**:
    - Assess the organization's workflows, current processes, and challenges.
    - Identify areas where Agile practices can bring value and address specific challenges.
- **Tailoring Agile Practices**:
    - Selectively choose Agile principles and practices that align with the organization's goals and context.

- Adapt and modify Agile ceremonies, artifacts, and roles to suit the team's dynamics and project requirements.

- **Customized Agile Framework**:
  - Create a customized Agile framework that reflects the organization's unique needs and culture.
  - This may involve combining elements from different Agile methodologies (Scrum, Kanban, XP, etc.) to create a hybrid approach.
- **Training and Education**:
  - Provide training and workshops to educate team members and stakeholders on Agile principles and practices.
  - Foster a shared understanding of Agile concepts and encourage collaboration in adapting Agile to the organization.
- **Iterative Improvement**:
  - Adopt an iterative approach to Agile implementation, where the organization continuously assesses, adapts, and improves its Agile practices.

    - Ask for feedback from stakeholders to identify areas for enhancement and make necessary adjustments.

- **Flexibility and Experimentation**:
    - Encourage teams to experiment with different Agile practices and techniques to find the best.
    - Embrace a culture of learning and adaptation, and consider the failures are the opportunities for growth.
- **Alignment with Organizational Goals**:
    - Ensure that Agile practices align with the organization's strategic objectives and business priorities.
    - Regularly revisit and refine Agile practices to ensure they contribute to the organization's overall success.

Organizations must adopt a customized approach that aligns with their unique context, culture, and goals to implement Agile effectively. One-size-fits-all solutions do not work, and it is important to dispel this myth.

CHAPTER 11

Scaling Agile

"Just Add More Teams for Scale"

The concept of Scaling Agile has gained a lot of attention in recent years, especially in the project and product management communities. Extending Agile practices beyond a single team to multiple teams, departments, or even across the entire organization has been viewed as a simple solution to handle larger projects or organizations. However, it's important to note that "just adding more teams for scale" oversimplifies the true essence of Agile scaling. Scaling Agile is not a one-size-fits-all approach or a quick fix for organizational challenges. It involves aligning efforts, improving collaboration, and maintaining Agile values and principles while working on complex projects or larger contexts. This means that it requires a good knowledge of Agile methodologies/frameworks and practices and also the needs and objectives of the organization. Scaling Agile is not merely about adding more teams. It's about developing an environment that helps collaboration, communication, and continuous improvement. It requires a cultural shift promoting transparency, trust, and empowerment, which can be challenging. Organizations need to ensure that they have the right infrastructure, tools, and processes to support Agile scaling and are willing to invest the time and resources needed to make it successful.

Organizations can reap the benefits of Agile scaling by investing the effort and resources needed to make Agile scaling successful, including improved efficiency, faster time to market, and better-quality products and services.

What Scaling Agile Means: Scaling Agile involves extending Agile practices beyond a single team to multiple teams, departments, or even across the entire organization. It's about aligning efforts, improving collaboration, and maintaining Agile values and principles while working on complex projects or in larger contexts.

What Scaling Agile Is Not: Contrary to popular belief, scaling Agile is not merely about adding more teams. It's not a one-size-fits-all approach or a quick fix for organizational challenges. Here are some misconceptions about scaling Agile:

Just Adding More Teams: Misconception: The belief that simply increasing the number of Agile teams will automatically lead to scalability.

Reality: Adding teams without addressing coordination, communication, and alignment can result in chaos, duplication of efforts, and diminished productivity.

Ignoring Organizational Structure: Misconception: Assuming that Agile practices seamlessly integrate with existing organizational hierarchies and structures.
Reality: Traditional hierarchies can hinder Agile's scalability. Without restructuring to support cross-functional teams and decentralized decision-making, Agile can become constrained.

Neglecting Culture and Mindset: Misconception: Treating Agile as a set of processes rather than a cultural shift.
Reality: Scaling Agile requires a shift in mindset towards collaboration, empowerment, and continuous improvement. This cultural aspect must be addressed to avoid resistance and ineffective implementation.

Examples of Agile Scaling Done Right:

Spotify's Agile Model:

Spotify has implemented an agile scaling strategy that involves restructuring its organization into several distinct units, including "squads," "tribes," "guilds," and "chapters." Squads are small cross-functional teams responsible for specific features or components, while tribes are collections of squads working on related areas. Guilds are communities of interest that span multiple squads, focusing on skill development and knowledge sharing. Chapters, however, are groups of individuals within a tribe who share the same role, such as software developers or designers.

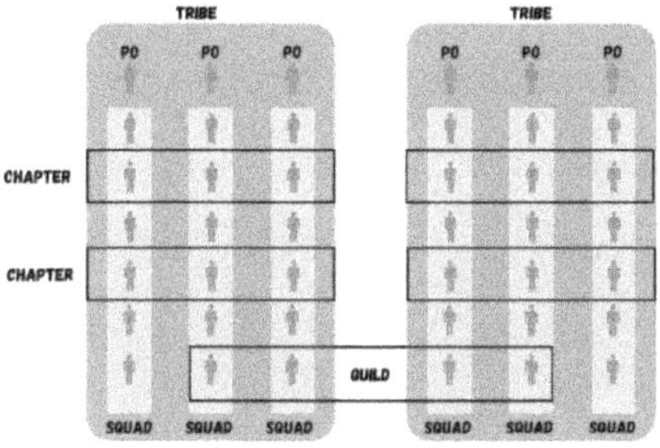

Fig 7: Spotify Org Structure

This unique structure promotes collaboration, autonomy, and innovation while aligning with Agile principles. Spotify has introduced new roles like "tribe leads" and "chapter leads" to provide guidance and support within these structures. This approach enables Spotify to effectively scale its agile practices across its organization, fostering adaptability and responsiveness to market demands.

It is noteworthy that Spotify's scaling was accomplished by not just adding more teams. They had to restructure their organizational structure, introduce new roles, and assign appropriate responsibilities. It is also important to understand that no matter how they restructure the basics, they still keep the core values and principles of Agile.

SAFe (Scaled Agile Framework):

SAFe, which stands for the Scaled Agile Framework, is a methodology designed to incorporate agile and lean principles across large organizations. It offers a structured approach to coordinate multiple agile teams working towards a common objective. By introducing various roles, ceremonies, and artifacts, SAFe facilitates collaboration, alignment, and delivery at scale. Key components of SAFe include Agile Release Trains (ARTs), which are cross-functional teams working together towards a shared mission, Program Increments (PIs) for planning and execution, and ceremonies like PI Planning, Inspect and Adapt, and Scrum of Scrums to ensure synchronization and continuous improvement. SAFe also emphasizes principles such as Lean thinking, systems thinking, and customer-centricity to drive value delivery and organizational agility. By adopting SAFe, enterprises can effectively manage complexity and achieve business agility while maintaining alignment and focus on delivering value to customers.

SAFe (Scaled Agile Framework) introduces several new roles to support its framework for scaling agile practices. These roles are essential for effective coordination, alignment, and delivery within the SAFe framework, enabling organizations to scale Agile practices across large and complex enterprises.

- Release Train Engineer (RTE): The RTE is a servant leader and facilitator for an Agile Release Train (ART). They lead and facilitate ART events and processes, ensure alignment between teams, and help remove impediments to progress.
- Product Management (PM): This role represents the voice of the customer and is responsible for defining and prioritizing features and enhancements to maximize the value delivered by the ART. Product Managers work closely with stakeholders to understand market needs and guide the product development process.
- System Architect/Engineering (SAE): SAEs are responsible for defining and helping the teams for technical direction of the solution. They collaborate with Agile teams to ensure architectural integrity and alignment with business objectives, promoting technical excellence and innovation.

- System Team: The System Team supports the ART by providing specialized skills, infrastructure, and tools needed to enable Agile teams to deliver value efficiently. They focus on architectural runway, tooling, and shared services to support the development efforts of Agile teams.
- Solution Train Engineer (STE): In larger organizations or when multiple ARTs need coordination, the Solution Train Engineer oversees the coordination and integration of multiple ARTs and solution-level events. They ensure alignment, facilitate cross-ART collaboration, and help resolve dependencies across the solution train.

These new roles can ensure alignment, coordination, and delivery within the SAFe framework. Organizations can benefit from these roles to scale Agile practices effectively.

Common Pitfalls in Scaling Agile:

Lack of Communication and Alignment:

Teams work in silos without regular communication or shared goals. Different Agile teams unknowingly work on conflicting features in a large organization, resulting in wasted efforts and delays.

Overly Prescriptive Frameworks:

Implementing a rigid, cookie-cutter approach to scaling Agile without considering unique organizational needs. Trying to force all teams to follow the same processes and ceremonies stifles creativity and adaptability.

Ignoring Feedback and Adaptation:

We must continuously assess and adjust Agile practices based on feedback and lessons learned. Persisting with a scaling approach that needs to be fixed diminishes team morale and project outcomes.

Matt: *Hey, Don, we need to talk about how we're scaling Agile in our organization. We're just adding more teams without considering the bigger picture.*

Don: *I've noticed that too. It feels like we're trying to scale Agile by replicating what works for one team across all teams.*

Matt: *Exactly, Don. Scaling Agile isn't as simple as adding more teams. It's about creating a system that enables multiple teams to work together towards common objectives.*

- *We need to ensure alignment, coordination, and collaboration across teams to achieve scale.*

Don: *But won't adding more teams automatically increase our productivity and output?*

Matt: *Not necessarily. Adding more teams without proper coordination can lead to inefficiencies, duplicated efforts, and conflicts.*

- *We need to focus on creating an ecosystem where teams can work independently yet collaboratively towards shared goals.*

Don: *I see what you mean. So, how do we ensure that our Agile scaling efforts are effective?*

Matt: *We can start by implementing Agile scaling frameworks like SAFe (Scaled Agile Framework) or LeSS (Large-Scale Scrum).*

- *These frameworks provide structures and practices for aligning and coordinating multiple Agile teams.*

Don: *That sounds promising. How do these frameworks help us scale Agile effectively?*

Matt: *SAFe, for example, offers concepts such as Agile Release Trains (ARTs) and Program Increments (PIs) to synchronise and align the work of multiple teams.*

- *LeSS focuses on simplifying the organizational structure and promoting self-managing, feature teams.*

Don: *That makes sense. So, it's about more than just adding more teams but creating a cohesive system for them to work together.*

Matt: *Exactly, Don. We want to avoid the "too many cooks in the kitchen" scenario and foster collaboration and shared understanding across teams.*

How to Scale your org…

Scaling Agile within an organization is not a simple or overnight task. It requires a systematic approach, which includes training stakeholders, preparing tools and technologies to support scaling, converting any legacy systems to support the required level of automation, piloting with one value stream, and then spreading the approach to the entire organization. Standard frameworks provide proven steps that can be followed to accomplish these tasks.

- **Implement Agile Scaling Frameworks:**
  - Adopt established Agile scaling frameworks such as SAFe, LeSS, or Nexus to provide structure and guidance for scaling efforts.

  - These frameworks offer practices, ceremonies, and roles for aligning and coordinating multiple Agile teams.
- **Feature Teams and Cross-Functional Collaboration**:
  - Encourage forming feature teams composed of members with diverse skills and expertise.
  - Foster cross-functional collaboration and knowledge sharing across teams to prevent silos and promote efficiency.
- **Alignment and Coordination**:
  - Establish regular alignment and coordination meetings, such as Scrum of Scrums or Kanban cadences.
  - Ensure that dependencies between teams are identified and addressed proactively.
- **Empowerment and Autonomy**:
  - Provide teams with the necessary directions to make decisions and self-organize within the larger scaled framework.
  - Empower teams to adapt practices and processes to suit their context while staying aligned with the organization's goals.
- **Continuous Improvement and Feedback**:

   - Create continuous improvement culture across the organization.
   - Encourage teams to provide feedback on scaling processes and practices and iterate on them for better effectiveness.
- **Leadership Support and Alignment**:
   - Ensure that leadership is aligned with Agile scaling efforts and provides support and resources as needed.
   - Leadership should actively champion the adoption of Agile principles and practices at scale.

Effective Agile scaling involves creating a shared vision and values that guide all teams' work and establishing clear roles, responsibilities, and communication channels. It also requires implementing scalable processes, tools, and metrics that enable teams to work together seamlessly and efficiently.

CHAPTER 12

Documentation

"Agile means no documentation."

One of Agile's key principles is prioritizing working software over comprehensive documentation, as the Agile Manifesto outlines. However, this does not mean that documentation is not valued or necessary. Instead, Agile emphasizes the importance of "just enough" documentation to facilitate communication, collaboration, and understanding within the team and with stakeholders.

Despite this, there is a common misconception that Agile discourages documentation entirely. This is not the case. Agile recognizes the value of documentation but seeks to balance producing comprehensive documentation and maintaining the flexibility to adapt to changing requirements. In this way, Agile supports the development of high-quality software that meets end-users needs. The role of documentation in Agile is multifaceted. Documentation is used to capture and communicate requirements, to track progress, and to provide a basis for testing and quality assurance. The primary documents in Agile are EPICs and User Stories. EPICs provide a high-level view of related user stories, while User Stories capture the user's perspective on a feature or requirement. Acceptance criteria, documented alongside User Stories, dictates the conditions to be met for the Story to be considered complete.

Documentation supports communication and collaboration within the team and plays a role in compliance and governance. Agile teams can perfectly fit into and support external regulations or standards, such as the Capability Maturity Model Integration (CMMI). CMMI models recommend planning project execution and audit verification of planned work, and Agile supports this.

Agile teams can maintain the flexibility to adapt to changing requirements by documenting the required details while still producing high-quality software that meets end-users needs.

Backlogs serve as a living document containing prioritized work items for the team. Because the traditional way of documentation goes into Word and Excel, which are artifacts, we don't feel like we have documentation either. This documentation's primary need and focus is to create an environment where flow doesn't impact. Assume you have a release at the start of the year, and at the end of the year, we need some enhancements. Without historical data, we won't achieve it without a waste of effort. In agile environments, tools capture the details that are just enough to keep this flow intact.

Effective documentation is a critical component of Agile methodology, and traceability is one of the key elements that ensures quick and easy access to information. This is achieved by linking user stories or requirements to implemented features within the release notes. The stories or releases are tagged within the code when checked in, making the entire process even more streamlined.

Matt: *Don, have you documented the recent requirement changes? We have a refinement Tomorrow, so we may go through them since we were told they are a priority.*

Don: *Oh wait, what do you mean by documenting it? We don't do documentation in Agile, do we?*

Matt: *That's a common myth. In Agile, we have documentation, but it's about creating what's necessary for effective communication and understanding.*

Don: *Can you give an example of Agile documentation that's crucial for our work?*

Matt: *Certainly. User stories and epics are foundational. They capture what the user needs and provide a clear path for development. In the present scenario, you may keep the stories updated with the requirement changes so we get them refined as we go along.*

Don: *Ah, so it's about defining the 'what' from the user's perspective.*

Matt: *Exactly. Acceptance criteria accompany these stories, detailing the conditions for success.*

Don: *I see. That helps ensure we're meeting the user's expectations.*

Matt: *Absolutely. And when we think about CMMI, it's not about drowning in documentation. It's about planning what we're going to do and documenting how we'll do it.*

Don: *That makes sense. So, Agile documentation is about keeping the communication flow while ensuring we're on track with our plans.*

Matt: *Precisely, Don. It's about having just enough documentation to support our Agile processes without getting lost in unnecessary details.*

Don: *Thanks, Matt. I appreciate the clarity. Agile documentation isn't about burdensome paperwork—it's about effective collaboration and progress tracking.*

Matt: *You're welcome, Don. Agile allows us to adapt our documentation to our needs, ensuring we deliver value efficiently and transparently.*

In traditional management methods, creating multiple documents before working on a project deliverable is common practice. To ensure that the project is well-documented, the process starts with creating a project charter, followed by a Business Requirement Document (BRD), Functional Requirement Specifications (FRS), System Requirement Specifications (SRS), Software Architecture Diagrams, Component Diagrams, and Entity Relationship Diagrams (ERD). This list can keep going until the source code is reached. All these documents are created, reviewed, and vetted by authorities to ensure that the released software meets the required features. However, this approach can be time-consuming and may delay the project timeline.

Moreover, in some cases, when the released software does not meet the required features, it becomes a huge problem, with many finger-pointing and blame games. To an extent, traditional documentation methods are created to ensure that other stakeholders review them, and when they fail, they also share the blame. Therefore, it is essential to balance document creation and actual project work to ensure that the project is completed on time and meets all the required features.

Creating Agile documentation requires a balance between providing enough documentation to facilitate communication and understanding without getting bogged down in unnecessary detail. The documentation should be clear, concise, and focused on providing essential information to team members. This process must involve collaboration between product owners, developers, testers, and stakeholders. Involving all stakeholders ensures a better understanding of the system and the ability to fix issues early in the project life cycle. Since the product is developed incrementally, surprises are greatly reduced. Any mistakes are caught early in the feedback process, providing a good opportunity to rectify them. Additionally, the documentation must be dynamic and evolve throughout the project as requirements change and new information emerges. This ensures the documentation stays relevant and up-to-date, providing the team with the information they need to make informed decisions.

Here is a quick comparison between traditional and agile project management methods, showing where the documentation goes for different phases and milestones. This is a sample list from Acme organization; you may do a mapping exercise as per your organization's PMO-defined artefacts.

Traditional Management	Agile
Requirements	
• Business Requirement Document • Functional Requirements Specification (FRS) • System Requirements Specification (SRS)	• Epics • User Stories • Acceptance Criteria
Project Planning	
Project Management Plan	Sprint Planning / Sprint Backlog
Work Breakdown Structure (WBS)	Backlog
Gantt Charts	Agile Roadmaps
Software Design	
Design Documents	Design Thinking Workshops (Stories gets updated accordingly)
Quality Assurance	
QA Plan & Metrics	Definition of Done
Monitor & Control	
Project Status Update Reports	Burndown / Burnup Charts, Control Chart, Sprint Reports
Trainings	
Training Materials	System demo, Hands-on Workshops

Quick References

Sprint Planning

- Ideal Duration: Typically lasts 4 hours for a 4-week sprint; shorter for shorter sprints.
- Timing: Sprint Planning occurs at the beginning of each sprint, immediately following the conclusion of the previous sprint.
- Frequency: Sprint Planning happens once per sprint, usually at the start of the sprint cycle.

Daily Standup (Daily Scrum)

- Ideal Duration: Generally kept to 15 minutes or less.
- Timing: The Daily Standup occurs at the same time and place every working day, preferably at the start of the workday.
- Frequency: Daily Standups occur daily throughout the sprint, providing regular updates and synchronization.

Sprint Review

- Ideal Duration: Typically lasts 1-2 hours for a 2-week sprint; longer for longer sprints.
- Timing: The Sprint Review takes place at the end of each sprint, following the completion of the sprint's work.

- Frequency: Sprint Reviews occur once per sprint, providing stakeholders with a chance to inspect the completed work and provide feedback.

Sprint Retrospective

- Ideal Duration: Usually around 1-2 hours, but may vary based on team size and sprint length.
- Timing: The Sprint Retrospective happens at the end of the sprint. Usually happens immediately after the Sprint Review and before the next Sprint Planning.
- Frequency: Sprint Retrospectives occur once per sprint, allowing the team to reflect on their processes and make improvements for the next sprint.

Backlog Refinement (Grooming)

- Ideal Duration: Can range from 1 to 2 hours, depending on the backlog size and complexity.
- Timing: Backlog Refinement sessions are held throughout the sprint, usually as needed to prepare upcoming backlog items for future sprints.
- Frequency: Backlog Refinement sessions occur regularly throughout the sprint, ensuring the backlog remains well-defined and prioritized for upcoming work.

Sprint Burndown Chart

The Burndown Chart visually represents the remaining work in the sprint backlog over time. This chart helps teams monitor their progress throughout the sprint and make necessary adjustments to ensure they meet their goals.

Velocity Chart

Velocity Chart showcases the amount of work the team completes in each sprint. By analyzing historical velocity, teams can forecast how much work they can accomplish in upcoming sprints, aiding in sprint planning and backlog refinement.

Cumulative Flow Diagram (CFD)

The Cumulative Flow Diagram (CFD) offers a comprehensive view of work items as they progress through different workflow stages. By analyzing the CFD, teams can identify bottlenecks, monitor flow efficiency, and optimize their workflow.

Control Chart

Control Chart visually represents the cycle time for issues (such as user stories or tasks). It displays the average time issues spent in each status or workflow state, allowing teams to track and analyze their workflow efficiency over time. The Control Chart typically a line graph, with the x-axis denoting time and the y-axis denoting the number of issues. The chart also includes control limits, such as upper and lower bounds, to highlight areas of process stability or variation.

Epic

Epic is a large piece of that can be broken into multiple smaller pieces, ideally into User Stories, that are more manageable pieces. Epics are typically high-level user requirements or features that span multiple sprints or iterations. They represent overarching goals or themes that contribute to the overall project vision. Epics are often used to organize and prioritize work in the product backlog and serve as a roadmap for development teams.

User Story

User Story describes a feature or requirement from an end-user perspective. It describes the user's wants and why rather than specifying technical details or implementation methods. User Stories usually follow a common template: "As a [user role], I want [goal], so that [benefit]." They serve as placeholders for conversations between stakeholders and development teams, facilitating collaboration and ensuring that the team's focus remains on delivering defined business value to users.

Task

A Task is a specific work that must be completed to fulfill a User Story or Epic. Tasks are smaller, actionable items that represent the steps necessary to implement a feature or requirement. They are typically created during sprint planning or backlog refinement sessions and are assigned to individual team members for execution. Tasks help break down larger pieces of work into manageable units and provide visibility into the progress of user stories and epics.

Sub-Task

A Subtask is a further breakdown of a User Story into even smaller, more granular pieces of work. Subtasks represent specific actions or activities required to complete a task and are often used to track progress in more detail. They can be created, assigned, and tracked independently within their parent tasks. They provide additional clarity and granularity, enabling teams to manage and monitor work more effectively.

Bugs/Defects

Bugs or Defects refer to issues or problems identified during testing or use of the software that deviate from expected behavior or specifications. They represent gaps in the system that deviates from the original requirements. These impact quality and reliability of the product. Bugs are typically logged, prioritized, and assigned to development teams for resolution. Tracking bugs and defects is essential for maintaining product quality and ensuring a positive user experience.

Definition of Done (DoD)

The Definition of Done is a set of criteria or standards to be met to declare the product increment is complete and ready for release. It encompasses all activities, quality checks, and conditions that need to be fulfilled for a user story, feature, or product backlog item to be considered "done" and potentially shippable. The DoD is established collaboratively by the development team, product owner, and other stakeholders at the beginning of a project or during the sprint planning process. It typically includes elements such as code review, unit testing, integration testing, documentation, user acceptance testing, and meeting acceptance criteria. Adhering to the Definition of Done ensures that the team delivers high-quality work consistently and maintains transparency about what constitutes a finished product increment.

Definition of Ready (DoR)

The Definition of Ready is a set of criteria or prerequisites that must be satisfied before a backlog item is selected for implementation during sprint planning. It serves as a checklist to ensure that items entering the sprint backlog are well-defined, actionable, and meet the team's standards for clarity and completeness. The DoR typically includes elements such as clear acceptance criteria, detailed requirements, dependencies identified, and any necessary resources or assets available. By establishing a clear Definition of Ready, teams can minimize ambiguity, reduce rework, and improve the efficiency of sprint planning and execution. It also fosters collaboration between the product owner and development team, helping to ensure alignment and understanding of expectations before work begins on a particular item.

Kanban Board

Kanban Board is a management tool used to visualize and manage work in progress in Kanban methodology. It typically consists of columns representing different workflow stages, such as To Do, In Progress, and Done. Each column contains cards representing individual work items, which move across the board as they progress through the workflow. The Kanban Board provides visibility into work status, limiting work in progress (WIP) and highlighting bottlenecks or areas where additional focus may be needed. It encourages continuous flow, promotes collaboration, and enables teams to identify and address issues quickly. Kanban Boards are flexible and can be customized to reflect the team's or project's specific workflow and priorities, making them adaptable to various contexts and environments.

Story Points

Story Points are the measurement units used in Agile project management to estimate the relative effort or complexity of completing a user story or task. Rather than focusing on precise time estimates, teams assign story points based on the perceived level of effort, complexity, and risk involved. Story Points help teams prioritize and plan their work, facilitating more accurate forecasting and capacity planning. They provide a common language for estimating and discussing work across the development team, fostering collaboration and alignment in Agile projects.

Planning Poker

Planning Poker is a collaborative estimation technique used in Agile project management, particularly in Scrum, to collectively estimate the effort required to complete user stories or tasks. During a planning poker session, team members individually assign story points to each item using a modified Fibonacci sequence or similar scale. After each team member has privately made their estimation, they reveal their estimates simultaneously. Any significant discrepancies in estimates prompt discussion among team members to share insights, clarify requirements, and align understanding. This iterative process continues until a consensus is reached on the estimated effort for each item. Planning Poker promotes engagement, transparency, and consensus-building within the team, resulting in more accurate and reliable estimates for planning and prioritization.

Acceptance Criteria

Acceptance Criteria describes the conditions or the requirements for a product or a feature to be accepted by the stakeholders, typically the product owner or customer. They define success for a user story or product backlog item and provide clear guidelines for the development team to ensure that the desired functionality or behavior is achieved. Acceptance Criteria are usually written concisely and precisely, often using "Given-When-Then" statements to describe the expected outcomes under certain conditions. They outline the functional, non-functional, and quality-related aspects that must be satisfied for the work to be considered complete. By defining Acceptance Criteria upfront, teams can ensure alignment with stakeholder expectations, facilitate effective collaboration, and deliver valuable, high-quality products that meet user needs.

Scrum Master

The Scrum Master is a role that facilitates the defined Scrum processes, identifies and removes impediments, and coaches the team on Agile principles and principles. They ensure the adherence of Agile practices and values, fosters collaboration, and focuses on delivering value. Additionally, the Scrum Master facilitates Scrum events such as sprint planning, daily stand-ups, sprint reviews, and retrospectives, helping the team to improve and adapt continuously.

Product Owner

The Product Owner represents stakeholders' interests, prioritizes the product backlog, and ensures value delivery. They define and prioritize user stories, gather requirements, and decide what features to include in each sprint or release. The Product Owner collaborates with the team to ensure that the product backlog is clear, understood, and aligned with the overall vision and goals of the project.

Lean

A philosophy and set of principles derived from Lean manufacturing, emphasizing the elimination of waste, optimizing flow, and continuous improvement.

www.ingramcontent.com/pod-product-compliance
Lightning Source LLC
LaVergne TN
LVHW021155160826
845679LV00024B/2134

* 9 7 9 8 8 9 3 6 3 9 4 0 7 *